FATE DID NOT LET ME GO

A MOTHER'S FAREWELL LETTER

Foreword by Stephen A. Ollendorff

Pelican Publishing Company
Gretna 2003

Photographs by Ivo Pervan
Contributing photographer: Alex Bemporad

Jacket and book designed by Nicole Sekora-Mendoza

Printed in the United States of America

Published by Pelican Publishing Company, Inc.
1000 Burmaster Street, Gretna, Louisiana 70053

This book is dedicated to the women in my life:
my grandmothers, Valli and Lucie; my mother Anne;
my wife Bjørg; and my granddaughter Kayla.

Stephen A. Ollendorff

With Special Thanks To:

Jakov Sedlar — his commitment and devotion
made this book possible; his inspiration created a
documentary based upon this book;

Ivo Pervan — his sensitivity to the letter is
demonstrated in the photographs;

Rabbi **Jack Bemporad** — our spiritual leader; and

George Mendoza — for his initial ideas.

VALLI OLLENDORFF

FOREWORD

This Letter from my paternal grandmother to my father was written, on August 24, 1942, at Rothenberg just prior to her being shipped to the Thereseienstadt concentration camp. She died there less than two months later. The Letter was discovered forty- three years later in a safe of the daughter of my grandmother's sister (Aunt Ella) in South America. The Letter was sent to my father who was 79 years old when he saw it for the first time. It was written in German and lovingly translated by my father, at my request, into English. Both versions appear at the end of this book.

The family always considered the Letter to be very private and only showed it to a few relatives and friends. When my father died on December 30, 1998, our family permitted our Rabbi to read the Letter at the eulogy. Its impact was so great that I realized it was much more than a private letter. It was a letter that would affect all people who read it.

In that spirit, our family has agreed to permit the publication of the Letter. In order to preserve its purity and remove all commercial motivation, all of the rights to the Letter have been donated to a tax-exempt charity whose purpose is to help promote human and religious understanding throughout the world.

Stephen A. Ollendorff

People named, or referred to, in the Letter

ARTHUR
(husband of Valli)

WOLFGANG
(son of Valli)

Picture not available. Died in Concentration Camp.

AUNT ELLA
(sister of Valli)

VALLI
(author of Letter)

ULRICH
(recipient of Letter
and son of Valli)

ANNE
(wife of Ulrich)

STEPHEN
(son of Ulrich and Anne,
grandson of Valli)

Tormensdorf
Rothenburg
Lusitz
Dated the 24th day of August, 1942

My beloved, my good boy,

*Within two days we are going away
from here, and the future lies so dark in
front of us that the thought comes up that
the new place will be the last one which we
reach on our migration.*

And if you my boy will hold this letter in your hands, then we are not chased from place to place, then all the suffering and restlesness will have an end.

Peace will then be around us and in us.

Be happy that I have this rest and this peace, my good boy, and don't be too sad. Believe me, this is the best that could happen.

I was, anyway, at the end of my life and the mother you knew, my beloved son, was not any more the same.

Too much suffering, too much psychological pain and stress came over me, and I cannot get over Wolfgang's death which will be one year on the 27th of August.

The suffering gets bigger day by day. The letters that I received from his friends speak of him with so much honor, friendship, respect and affection. The letters show me only what he became and still could have become and achieved, and how much joy, spiritual wealth and wisdom he had and passed onto others. His letters to his father and me contained touching gratitude for his childhood and youth.

Also, you, my beloved boy, can carry the knowledge through your life that you through all your life were a source of purest joy for your parents, and that you, even in the times in which you like other boys of the same age were difficult, never gave your character cause for annoyance or hurt feelings.

I wish your life will go from success to success, my beloved boy, and that you stay so good, so modest, and so grateful for all the good and beautiful things like you did already as a child.

We wish for you to have with your child as much joy as we had with you. May the blessings, which I pray for you, come true. And I wish to your Anne, your loyal life partner, with whom you brought us a beloved daughter in our home, and your child a happy and joyful life together.

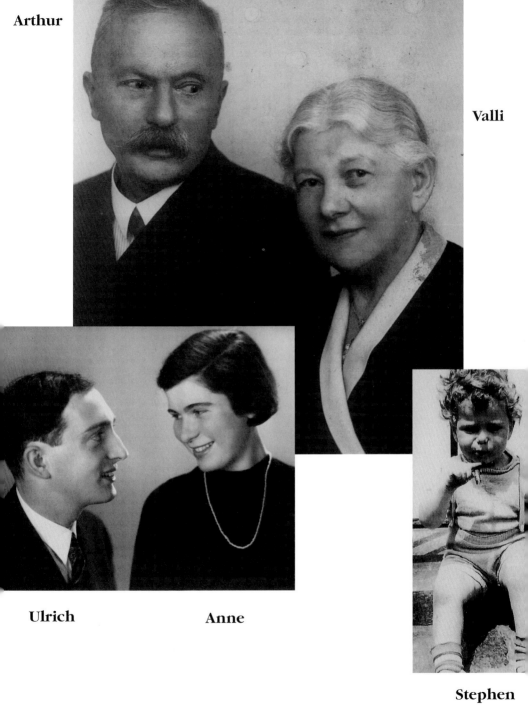

Arthur

Valli

Ulrich

Anne

Stephen

The fact that I could not be a witness to your life in America was much more sad for me than you believed, my boy.

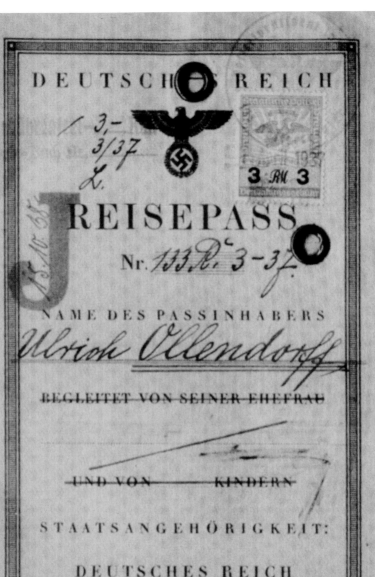

DEUTSCHES REICH

REISEPASS

Nr. 133 R. 3-37.

NAME DES PASSINHABERS

Ulrich Ollendorff

BEGLEITET VON SEINER EHEFRAU

UND VON   KINDERN

STAATSANGEHÖRIGKEIT:

DEUTSCHES REICH

Dieser Paß enthält 32 Seiten

All your letters born by a deep child's love called me to you and the joy of seeing you again, and the echo of the longing, and the possibility of living with you made me try to do everything necessary to come to you.

If I did not write so often from all of my longing for you, it was done from love to you, because I believed it was better for you.

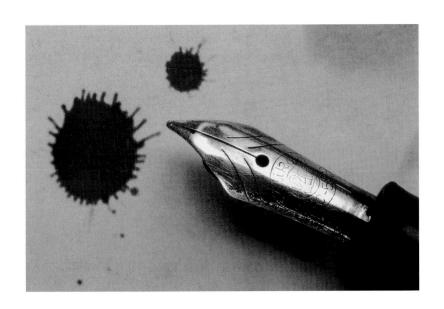

Also, today I repeat to you and
I know that you will understand me,
I was and I am daily happy even
longing very much for you and your life.

However, fate did not let me go.

I was a necessity for Aunt Ella and I think that will console you. I wish it so very much. And now my beloved boy, I will take leave from you.

I will thank you a thousand times for all the love, for all the gratitude, for all the joy and sunshine which you brought into your father's and my life, starting from the day of your birth.

Arthur and Ulrich

May the memory of your parent's house and your childhood shine like a bright, lucky star over you, my beloved, good, precious boy.

Mother

Aunt Ella, Valli & Arthur

A brief background of Valli and the family

Unfortunately, details of my father's family are sketchy since the entire side of that family died in concentration camp or through the passage of time. None of them (except my father) survived WW II. My parents left Germany with me in November of 1938. I was three and a half months old. I rarely discussed the intimate details of my father's family with my father due to the emotional distress it would cause. With my father's death in December, 1998, a lot of the details of his family are no longer available. Some of the details were supplied by Yad Vashem and Theresienstadter Gedenk/Buch.

Valli Ollendorff — author of the Letter. Born in 1874 in Breslau, Germany. Her maiden name was Valli Alexander. She married Dr. Arthur Ollendorff on October 28, 1902 and bore three sons, Gerhard, Wolfgang and my father Ulrich. The entire family was raised in Breslau. All of her personal dignity and traits are best expressed in the Letter and no further words are necessary. She was arrested in Breslau and arrived in the Theresienstadt concentration camp on August 31, 1942 with her sister (referred to in the letter as Aunt Ella). Valli died there on October 16, 1942. Aunt Ella died there on December 2, 1942.

Dr. **Arthur Ollendorff** — born in 1868. He was the husband of Valli. He was a doctor, a dentist and an entrepreneur. He served as an Colonel in the German army during WW I. He died of a heart attack before Valli was taken to concentration camp. His memory is sustained through the naming of his great-grandchild Arthur, who is a doctor at the University of Cincinnati.

Gerhard Ollendorff — born in 1903, in Breslau, Germany. He was the oldest son of Valli. Little is known about him other than he disappeared in 1939 and was presumed eliminated by the Nazis in the 1940s.

Dr. **Ulrich Ollendorff** — born in 1906, in Breslau, Germany. My father married my mother, Anne, on September 15, 1936. He was a practicing ophthalmologist in Berlin, Germany. My parents and I fled Germany on November 11, 1938 (the day after Krystallnacht) and settled in America. My father became a successful ophthalmologist in New York, establishing a practice of several hundred thousand patients in upper Manhattan. He died on December 30, 1998. His achievements are honored at the Eye Institute of Columbia University through a lectureship series and a diagnostic center, both established in his name. His greatest trait was his humanity. His role model was his mother, Valli.

Wolfgang Ollendorff — born in 1910, in Breslau, Germany. He was the youngest son of Valli. He was reputed to be a brilliant scientist. Wolfgang was very active in the underground but was finally captured in Holland. Notwithstanding extreme torture, it has been reported to us he refused to disclose any other members of the underground movement. He was shot in the concentration camp in Mauthausen on August 27, 1941, while trying to escape.

Anne Ollendorff — my mother and the wife of Dr. Ulrich Ollendorff, born in 1916 in Berlin, Germany. When my parents arrived with me in America in December, 1938, my father had to learn English and study for the medical boards in New York. Due to financial hardship, my mother and I lived with

Professor and Mrs. Sarvis, a wonderful Quaker couple, in Delaware, Ohio for a year. My mother worked in a factory, with me by her side. In 1946, my mother gave birth to my brother David. My mother is still living in the home we grew up in, enjoying her family and friends. Her strength in the face of pain and crisis is legendary.

Stephen A. Ollendorff — born in 1938 in Berlin, Germany. A graduate of the College and Law School of Columbia University. My greatest pleasures in life are my wife, Bjorg, my sons, Arthur and Robert, Candice (Arthur's wife) and my granddaughter Kayla. I am a practicing lawyer and businessman in New York. However, my main goal is to help achieve the demise of anti-semitism. To that end, I am the President of The Ollendorff Center for Religious and Human Understanding, Inc.

Dr. **David Ollendorff** — born in 1946, in New York City. My brother, David, is a practicing physician in Chicago, Illinois. By becoming a doctor, he has carried on the family tradition, a source of great joy to my parents. He is married to Riitta, and they have one daughter, Linda.

Tormensdorf
Rothenburg
Lusitz
Am 24.8.1942

Mein geliebter, mein guter Junge!

In zwei Tagen gehen wir von hier fort, u. die Zukunft liegt so dunkel vor uns, dass der Gedanke nicht fern liegt, dass der neue Aufenthaltsort der letzte ist, den wir auf unserer Wanderung erreichen, u. wenn Du, mein Junge, diese Zeilen in Händen hältst, dann sind wir nicht mehr vertrieben von Ort zu Ort, dann hat alles Leid ein Ende, auch die Ruhelosigkeit u. Frieden ist um uns u. in uns. Gönne mir diese Ruhe u. diesen Frieden, mein guter Junge u. sei nicht zu traurig, glaube mir, es ist so das Beste. Ich stand ja so am Ende meines Lebens, u. die Mutter, die Du kanntest, mein geliebter Sohn, die war ich nicht mehr; zu viel Schweres, zu viel Leid u. Aufregungen sind über mich gekommen u. über Wolfgangs Tod, der sich am 27. Aug. jährt, komme ich nicht hinweg, der Schmerz wird täglich grösser, u. die Briefe, die ich von seinen Kameraden erhalten habe u. die mit so viel Verehrung, Zuneigung u. Anerkennung von ihm sprechen, zeigen mir nur, was aus ihm schon geworden war u. noch mehr hätte werden können, wie viel Freude, seelischen Reichtum u. geistiges Können er hatte u. verbreitete. Seine Briefe an Vater u. mich waren von einer rührenden Dankbarkeit für Kindheit u. Jugend. – Auch Du, mein geliebter Junge, kannst das Bewusstsein durch Dein Leben tragen, dass Du Dein ganzes Leben hindurch für Deine Eltern ein Quell reinster Freude warst, u. dass Du auch in den Zeiten, in denen Du wie andre Jungen in gewissem Alter schwierig warst, nie Dein Charakter Anlass zu

Aerger oder Verstimmung gab. Möge Dein Leben von Erfolg zu Erfolg gehen, mein geliebter Junge, u. Du dabei so gütig, so bescheiden, so dankbar für alles Gute u. Schöne bleiben, wie Du es schon als Kind warst; mögest Du an Deinem Kinde so viel Freude haben, wie wir an Dir hatten; möge der Segen, den ich auf Dein Haupt herabflehe, in Erfüllung gehen u. Deine Arme, Deine treue Lebensgefährtin, mit der Du mir eine geliebte Tochter ins Haus geführt hast, mit Dir u. Deinem Kinde vereint ein glückliches frohes Leben führen. Dass ich nicht Zeuge Eures Lebens in Amerika sein konnte, war viel trauriger für mich, als Du glaubtest, mein Junge; all Deine Briefe, die getragen von heisser Kindesliebe mich zu euch riefen, riefen in mir das Echo der Sehnsucht u. die Freude auf ein Wiedersehen, auf ein Miteuchleben hervor u. veranlassten, dass ich immer sofort alles Notwendige tat, um zu Euch zu kommen; wenn ich Euch von meiner Bangigkeit nicht so oft schrieb, so war es aus Liebe zu Euch, weil ich glaubte, es wäre besser für Euch. Auch heute sage ich Euch wieder, u. ich weiss, dass Ihr mich versteht, ich war u. bin täglich glücklich, wenn auch von heisser Sehnsucht nach Euch u. Eurem Leben erfüllt, dass das Schicksal mich nicht gehen liess, ich war für Tante Ella eine Notwendigkeit u. ich denke, das wird Euch trösten; ich wünschte es so sehr. Und nun, mein geliebter Junge, will ich Abschied von Dir nehmen, will Die tausend Mal danken für alle Liebe, für alle Dankbarkeit, für all die Freude u. den Sonnenschein, den Du in Vaters u. mein Leben gebracht hast vom Tage Deiner Geburt an. Die Erinnerung an Dein Elternhaus u. Deine Kindheit leuchte wie ein strahlender, glückbringender Stern über Dir, meinem geliebten, guten teuren Jungen.

Mutterchen.

Tormensdorf
Rothenburg
Lusitz
Dated the 24th day of August, 1942

My beloved, my good boy,

Within two days we are going away from here, and
the future lies so dark in front of us that the thought
comes up that the new place will be the last one
which we reach on our migration. And if you my boy
will hold this letter in your hands, then we are not
chased from place to place, then all the suffering and
restlesness will have an end. Peace will then be around
us and in us. Be happy that I have this rest and this
peace, my good boy, and don't be too sad. Believe me,
this is the best that could happen. I was, anyway, at the
end of my life and the mother you knew, my beloved
son, was not any more the same. Too much suffering,
too much psychological pain and stress came over me,
and I cannot get over Wolfgang's death which will be
one year on the 27th of August. The suffering gets
bigger day by day. The letters that I received from his
friends speak of him with so much honor, friendship,
respect and affection. The letters show me only what
he became and still could have become and achieved,
and how much joy, spiritual wealth and wisdom he
had and passed onto others. His letters to his father
and me contained touching gratitude for his childhood
and youth. Also, you, my beloved boy, can carry the
knowledge through your life that you through all your
life were a source of purest joy for your parents, and
that you, even in the times in which you like other
boys of the same age were difficult, never gave your

character cause for annoyance or hurt feelings. I wish your life will go from success to success, my beloved boy, and that you stay so good, so modest, and so grateful for all the good and beautiful things like you did already as a child. We wish for you to have with your child as much joy as we had with you. May the blessings, which I pray for you, come true. And I wish to your Anne, your loyal life partner, with whom you brought us a beloved daughter in our home, and your child a happy and joyful life together.

The fact that I could not be a witness to your life in America was much more sad for me than you believed, my boy. All your letters born by a deep child's love called me to you and the joy of seeing you again, and the echo of the longing, and the possibility of living with you made me try to do everything necessary to come to you. If I did not write so often from all of my longing for you, it was done from love to you, because I believed it was better for you. Also, today I repeat to you and I know that you will understand me, I was and I am daily happy even longing very much for you and your life. However, fate did not let me go. I was a necessity for Aunt Ella and I think that will console you. I wish it so very much. And now my beloved boy, I will take leave from you. I will thank you a thousand times for all the love, for all the gratitude, for all the joy and sunshine which you brought into your father's and my life, starting from the day of your birth. May the memory of your parent's house and your childhood shine like a bright, lucky star over you, my beloved, good, precious boy.

Mother

Sculpture in Mauthausen where Wolfgang was shot trying to escape